SYNCHRONIZED WITH NATIONAL EDUCATION POLICY -2020.

REFORMATIONS IN SCHOOLING.

Fix Education to Eradicate Poverty, Build the Economy and Become Superpowers.

SAMPAT DANIEL

Book Title: "REFORMATIONS IN SCHOOLING".

Author: SAMPAT DANIEL

Self Published by: SAMPAT DANIEL   mailto:admin@airref.co.in
AirRef Engineers and Consultants:- Mumbai, India

ASIN: B08FHD8429
ISBN: 978-93-5419-657-1

1st Published 2020 – Paperback printing.

Cover design by Fiverr   : Printed in India.

POTHI.Com (Print on Demand) a division of Mudranik Technologies Pvt Ltd, # 634, 5th Main Road, Indiranagar 2nd stage, Bangalore – 560038 Ph: 080 48661923; info@pothi.com www.pothi.com

DEDICATED TO

This book is dedicated to my daughter Aksheta Hannah for her desire and dedication to educating young children in the world in primary schools K-3. She had left India to pursue her studies in Australia in Masters in Teaching (Primary) though having M.Sc in Environmental Science, as she was keen to teach children in schools. Hope this book will inspire her desire to educate the lower strata of school children in the world.

Her passion has prompted me to author this book to bring a change in the education system, especially in my country in India.

PART I:

HOW NATURAL DISASTERS IN THE WORLD ARE EFFECTING EDUCATION.

The story of Dr. Radha Binod Pal.

Prevailing education system.

How to protect and keep Children engaged in studies.

Different types of schools in operation.

Different types of Boards used in Private and Government schools.

The knowledge gap between Private Public Schools and Government schools.

Children's right to quality education.

PART II:

EDUCATION SYSTEM AND GOVERNMENT POLICIES IN INDIA.

Modern Education system in India.

Different types of schooling in operation.

Different education boards used by the government and private schools.

Bridging the knowledge gap between Government schools and Private schools students.

All children have the right to high-quality education.

Teacher remunerations and assessments.

<u>PART III:</u>

FORMAL EDUCATION SYSTEM PREVAILING IN THE WORLD.

<u>PART IV:</u>

FACTORS AFFECTING PERFORMANCE OF EDUCATION IN POOR COUNTRIES.

Lack of formal education system and infrastructure.

Socio-economic factors affecting education.

Government and Leaders' willingness to change.

<u>PART V:</u>

Education in the industrialized world.

Education in the Industrial and economically developed countries.

Lack of need to adapt to the changes in the world, slowing the growth of the countries.

PART VI:

Reformation is a Continuous process in school education.

Adapt the education system according to the needs.

Alternative methods of teaching.

Governments, Educational leaders, authorities must support the change in the education system.

Transition and building alliances with different parties in the field of education.

Build infrastructure facilities for effective collaboration, teamwork, and networking in schools.

Enhanced learning through the use of digital technology.

Infrastructure resources and transitioning of school teaching.

Principals and Practices of collaborative roles and responsibilities.

Building alliances with Government and Private Universities In the World.

<u>**PART VII:**</u>

Reformations in schools in India

Adaptive Modulation School Learning.

Community Learning Schools and Colleges.

Non-Collegiate education.

Blended Learning Schools.

Student's assessments and grading.

Transformation Learning Schools.

Pre-Schools in India (Anganwadi Centers).

Teacher Eligibility Tests.

Teacher Assessments and Remunerations.

Private stakeholders and Government Funding.

Parents and Local Larders' Co-operation.

Interview with Faculty, case study, and Examples for overall improvement in teaching methods in Schools.

Benefits of adaptive modulation learning schools and colleges

Elder's Education System in India

Education at Lower Cost

Teacher Training & Remunerations.

A win-win situation for all stakeholders

LIST OF CHARTS AND TABLES.

Acknowledgment

As always, thanks first and foremost to the many thousands of incredible people who have shared with me over the years the lessons of their experiences in the workplace.

I want to thank all the Principals, Professors, Teachers, and school administrators, who have expressed so much confidence in my work and who have given me the opportunity to learn from real issues they deal with and solve daily.

Many thanks as well to Dr. Sameer Jadhave – Professor at the IIT, Bombay. Mr. Som Bathla for guiding me in preparing and writing this book, and also the excellent team of author's supporting me from the AFC group.

To my family and friends, I owe you my deep thanks for being you and for allowing me to be who I am, to proceed on my journey of writing, and on the mission of reform schooling to uplift the poor and the deserving lives.

PREFACE:

Like many people on their journey, I found my way into sales, then management, production, administration, and eventually entrepreneurship and consultancy. Over time, I began to notice a consistent and predictable pattern and principles that seemed to accompany all business success, the ones who are not satisfied or contended in their achievements or their desires and dreams always seem to unfulfilled and constantly trying to achieve, prove or disrupt the normal, in doing so they have made discoveries, invented many things, people trying to reaching different planets, created new products and services for a better life, today, in the technological world, there are virtual meeting, remote medical operations, the world has come closed as never before.

I believe that life is the most precious and wonderful of all gifts, and to see its growth to the full potential and bloom itself and transfer into the next generations is my desire and purpose of this book. It is to liberate individual potential by giving them the best education, equal opportunities to the rich and the poor in every country.

It is the most beautiful time to be alive, there have never been more opportunities for more people to accomplish more their goals, both personally and professionally, than exists today, and the situation is getting better by the day

Today strategies and techniques for achieving success at every level of education, and in every activity of life, are more widely available and proliferating more rapidly than at any other time in human history. We all benefit from them by seizing them and applying them in our lives, knowledge is cumulative, once it exists, it does not cease to exist at any time. Therefore, it should become available to more and more people and grow exponentially in teaching practices.

The education system and method of teaching in many developed nations, with well-established education systems, are failing to impart the education that is required for the present situations for the growth, stability, and innovation in the country, for the people to have a better lifestyle. Countries who have innovated new methods of teaching and with stringent assessments at the early stage of the child education have leapfrogged to become powerful nations, like China, Rwanda, Guyana in Africa, Thailand and partially India, more because of the students opting for higher education abroad, the GER still being below 50% which hold 40% of the economy in the World.

This book brings about the change in the education system to foster the growth and give equal opportunities for every child, has a right to education for every citizen and the Governments primary responsibility to further it, in continuously supporting the weak and the venerable in every region, and giving support, providing best methods and facilities for the growth of the child and imparting knowledge through experiential learning practiced in the world using the latest technology and innovative methods.

Thankfully the Indian Government has embarked on major reforms in education system In National Education Policy – 2020 which was unveiled on 29th July 2020, after 34 years of reforms, with many major changes in the policy, especially changing the structure of schools to 5+3+3+4, a clear shift and the focus majorly on the pre-schooling using Anganwadi Centers, if implemented, will transform and empower the children to dream big. The ambition plans of GER of 100% from the current levels of 50% and also 50% in higher education from the levels of 25.6%. Is a real challenge. The policy also opens up for foreign universities to enter in Indian space, which will give a competitive edge and improve the standard of education at the university level.

The book also addresses the concerns and reforms in another area, Teacher Student Ration, Teacher Education, Remunerations, and Structure of Growth, the opportunities for private players to open up in Core Learning Schools, for holistic growth of the students learning. It also addresses the issue of Elder's Life Supporting Education.

I believe that if implemented as suggested in the book, in the next 20 years, one generation of student life can completely transform and bring a better lifestyle, will empower people of individual rights and responsibilities, and to outflow all forms of social discrimination. I believe that life is the most precious and wonderful of all gifts. Education will make a better place for life for all living beings.

INTRODUCTION

Education brings Prosperity.

This book is for all those who are in the education profession, Governments, Organizations, Leaders, Educators, Professionals, Entrepreneur, Teachers, Employees, Parent, and Students, to discover how you can change the education system and also be a part of the change if we can fix education, we can fix poverty for all future generations.

When you educate an elder, you bring in happiness and poetry, when you educate a youth you empower him with the knowledge and skills to lead a contented life and when you educate a child you change a generation and empower them to change the world for a better place to live in.

The book proposes changes from the grass route level at the Pre-primary schooling starting from the Anganwadi centers to the Universities.

AIMS OF THIS BOOK

One has only to look at a large number of books on the school curriculum, teaching methods, teacher guidance and support to the students and practicing administrators, rather than the failing school standards in the current education system, which is not able to address this issue.

The present book is written to fulfill the gaps that the author found when trying to assign suitable books for the Leaders, Governments, and experienced Educators to bring about the reforms in schooling. Generations are passing by in poverty, the standard of education deteriorating, and the students' learning skills are not job-ready.

There is an urgent need to reform school education systems in many countries; the GER is only 20% to 56% in most of the underdeveloped and developing countries. Every child has a right to education, but the system denies them the opportunity to dream big and create a future for a better life.

This book brings about changes in the structure of education and the utilization of resources for better learning to bridge the gap between the charter schools and private-public schools.

There are charts and graphic design used to illustrate to the reader the proposed methods of change for inclusive studies for all the students in a rural area and in cities. The suggestions in the book for restructuring and utilizing the existing resources in schools with a considerable reduction in the budgets of the State and Central Governments also provide the best facilities to all students from all schools. The private players in education can also implement their knowledge and skills in core competence than trying to be masters in all fields.

The book is designed to be read either as a whole or for individual chapters, Summary at the end of the book is there to help the reader re-cap the book contents for easy implementations as suggested in the book. The aim through the book is to help the Governments, Leaders, and Administrators to understand the problems, and knowing the advantages and disadvantages of different ways of dealing with them and implement to bring about the change in the education system, to bridge the gap in learning between the Government schools and the Private educational Institutes to eradicate poverty and given an opportunity everyone to excel in life.

Part 1:

The story of Dr. Radha Binod Pal:

*"The best anti-poverty program is a world-class education." – **Barack Obama**.*

*"Education is indeed and effectually the best way of the poor to escape not only poverty but to also kill illiteracy and ignorance and unawareness of individual rights and responsibilities and to outflow all forms of social discrimination." - **Rachida Zoubid of Md V University of Rabat.***

Knowledge gives children the power to dream of a better future and the confidence needed to pursue a full education, which in turn will help a generation.

There are huge gaps economically between the rich countries, developing and the poor countries in the World, the struggle continues with many of the countries to bridge the gap, some even drifting backward, many Western European countries who were economically well off, are now losing their ground. We have to answer why poor nations are not able to bridge the gap with the rich and developed nations economically? And the answer is simply, lack of political will to implement the right to educate their citizens of the country. Because of the lack of opportunities to educate the children, the poor nations continue to struggle. The countries with a good education system and with facilities for mass education of their children are prospering today.

Every country's future is totally dependent on the educated children of the nation, for their growth of Industry, Innovation, and sustainability.

This is the story of a poor Indian in the 19th century, who was fortunate enough to be educated, has transformed the thinking of the world, and brought prosperity to himself and the Country.

Know Dr. Radha Binod Pal, a Judge of India.

Born in 1886 in the Kumbh of the East Bengal, now called Bangladesh, his mother made a living by taking care of the household and their cow, for feeding the cow, Radha used to take the cow to the land near a local primary school. When the teacher thought in school, Radha used to listen from outside one day, the school inspector came to visit the school from the city. He asked some questions to the students after entering the class. Everyone was silent, Radha said from outside the classroom window…

"I know the answers to all your questions."And he answered all the questions one by one. Inspector said, "Wonderful, which class do you read?"

The answer came, "I do not read. I graze cows",

Everyone was shocked to hear that. Calling the head teacher, the school inspector instructed the boy to take admission in the school as well as provide some stipend.

This is how the education of Radha Binod Pal started. Then after passing the school finals with the highest number in the district, he was admitted to Presidency College. After taking M.Sc from the University of Calcutta, he studied law again and got the Doctorate title. In the context of choosing the opposite of two things, he once said, "Law and mathematics are not so different after all."

Then one day on 12th November 1948, Tokyo Trials (International Military Tribunal for the Far East), are going on in a huge garden house on the outskirts of Tokyo, the trial of fifty-five Japanese war criminals including Japan's then Prime Minister- Hideki Tojo, after losing WW II.

Of these, twenty–eight people have been identified as Class-A (crimes against peace), war criminals. If proved, the only punishment is the "death penalty."

Eleven international judges from all over the world are announcing... "Guilty"..."Guilty"..."Guilty"........suddenly one thundered, "Not Guilty!"

A silence came down in the hallway, who was this lone dissenter?

His name was Radha Binod Pal, a judge from India.

In his convincing argument to the rest of the jurists, he signified that the Allies (Winners of WW II), also violated the principles of restraint and neutrality of international law. In addition to ignoring Japan's surrender hints, they killed two hundred thousand innocent people using nuclear bombardment. The judge was forced to drop many of the accused from Class-A to B, after seeing the logic written on twelve hundred thirty–two Class-B war criminals were saved by him from the sure death penalty. His verdict in the international court gave him and India a world-famous reputation.

Dr. Radha Binod Pal's name is remembered in the history of Japan. In Tokyo, Japan, he has a museum and a statue in the Yasukuni shrine.

Japan University has a research center in his name.

He is the author of many books related to law in India. Dr. Pal was elected to the United Nations International Law Commission, where he served from 1958 to 1966. He was also one of the key persons who drafted the Indian Income-tax act of 1922, He was one of the architects of modern Indian Law system, and he worked as Vice-Chancellor of Calcutta University in 1944.

Ref: **"Shankar Chatterjee"**

There are many such inspiring true stories in many countries, which have changed lives only due to education, today the opportunities to educate the poor and downtrodden in economically poor countries is so grieved that we are losing good talent and generations are passing bye.

We need immediate reformation in our education system, which can impact the entire country and giving opportunities to every child to be educated with the best of the facilities, be it in a rural area or the Big Cities.

Divide between the poor and the rich countries continue. Why poor nations are not able to bridge the gap with the rich and developed nations economically simply because of lack of opportunities to educate the children of the nations, the country with good education facilities and mass education of their children are builders of the future of the country.

To fix poverty, first, we need to fix the education system and educate the children to cope with the current development in technological advancements.

Today's scenario with regards to the education system.

There has been a drastic transformation in Schooling in the current days of education, World over, after the COVID-19, Pandemic affecting the world, with schools being closed for almost 4 to 6 months in many countries all across the world, as many schools are shut to avoid infection to the teachers and school children, which has affected all countries rich, developing and the poor, irrespective of the cultures, creed, color, or their food habits, be it in Europe, Latin America, Asia, and African.

The Covid-19 virus, which originated in WUHAN in China, has quickly spread across the globe like wildfire, and many countries have imposed lockdown to take precautionary measures against the spread of the virus, restricting movements, closing down markets, commercial operations, workplaces, schools & colleges.

This has affected the entire economy of all countries, putting tremendous pressure on governments to take alternative methods of reviving the economy; however, the most affected sector is in schools and colleges.

As these institutions were closed, there is no revenue generation to governments, due to which the entire schools and colleges all across the world had been shut as most of the schools are funded by the Governments giving free education to the children.

In effect, the children became venerable to child abuse at home, sexual harassment due to lack of direction, and the education system had not adapted to the changes, the children lost their year of schooling.

This has prompted many schools to change to new methods of teaching in schools; one of the quick adaptations was online studies as the technology was available, but mostly in higher education. Going online teaching the students to learn from home to cope up with the studies has become a challenge, however, to keep up to their studies, especially to complete the curriculum and conduct examinations for the students to pursue their carrier.

The governments are put into tremendous pressure on schools and colleges to complete the academic year, as the infrastructure to complete the courses is not in place and the schools and colleges, with in-person classes not possible due to the closure of schools and college the results were announced based on their class assessments.

Many schools and colleges in reputed universities and colleges across the globe have incomplete courses with total uncertainty with the year going by, the student's life has completely changed with school children becoming restless, indiscipline and losing the early learning of discipline in life is making them venerable to bad habits, pedophilia, pornography, child trafficking, and child abuse at home.

How to protect and keep Children engaged in studies.

It is now imperative that we transform immediately into new teaching methods in schools and colleges and the form of attending their classes.

With the fast developments in the field of science and technology changing at a rapid pace, it is now time for us to combine the Online teachings and in-person schooling to usher the teaching methods to complete their curriculum, in many countries this is being done effortlessly, utilizing the best teaching techniques and methods in schooling in remote areas, whether poor or rich countries across the world, with the assistance of the Local Governments.

PART II:

Education and Government policies in India:

"The research has a conclusion that we in India are expecting too little of our students and that we need to work together to enact the kinds of reforms that will enable our schools to help all youngsters reach their maximum potential."

India has evolved from the early teaching of-Gurukula system of education, which was limited to a few students who were accepted by the Guru who taught Sanskrit, Holy Scriptures Mathematics and Metaphysics. The student and the teacher had a strong bond as the students lived with the Guru helping in all the activities at home. The drawbacks were that they were limited students, and the education was for the preferred community. It had its own drawbacks, with limited students, informal education systems of assessments, and not recognized admissible schools, which are prevalent even today in some countries, like India, Indonesia, and Burma.

The modern education system in India today.

The modern school system was brought to India, including the English language, originally by Lord Thomas Babington Macaulay in the 1830s. The subjects were science, maths, languages, and most of the teaching was classroom teaching. Other extra-curricular activities and the link with nature was broken, which was evident in Gurukula.

The early schooling was operated by the Churches, and missionaries from England, Scotland, Italy, and Portugal, some of such schools run by the Nuns from Italy. They operated the schools built by the Railways for their staff children, where I was educated in my primary schooling. There were also many religious organizations operating schools for their communities. All these schools follow the guidelines of the state boards or central boards for their curriculums and assessments.

After a century of school education there were reforms in school systems of having a unified standard of teaching in all schools with a boards exams to assess the performance of the student, in this regards the Uttar Pradesh board was set up in India in the year 1921 with jurisdiction over Rajputana, Central India, and Gwalior, eventually by 1952 a new board was constituted in the name of Central Board of Secondary Education (CBSE).

It was the function of the board to decide on things like curriculum, textbooks, and examinations system for schools affiliated under it. Today there are thousands of schools affiliated to the Board both within India and in many countries like Afghanistan and Zimbabwe...

The primary education in all state governments is free, and under the constitution, article 45 Primary educations are the fundamental right of all the citizens. And the government spends around 4.1% of its GDP, which is very low compared to many countries that spend a maximum of up to 7% of the GDP.

The government in its resent, proposed changes and brought about the National Common Minimum Programmers (NCMP)

1. To progressively increase expenditure on education to about 6% of GDP by 2028.

2. To make the Right to education a fundamental right for all children in the age group of 6-14 Years.

3. To universalize educations through its flagship programmers such as Sarva Siksha Abhiyan and Mid-day Meals.

The Central Advisory Board of Education (CABE), continues to play a lead role in the evolution and monitoring of educational policies and programmers

There are also other bodies for key roles in developing policies and programmers, the NCERT – National Council for Educational Research and Training, the State Council for Educational Research and Training (SCERT) these bodies essentially propose educational reforms, curricula, pedagogical schemes and evaluation methodologies to the state department of education.

There are different boards under the NCSERT, the CBSE board is set up for the central government employees children as their jobs are transferable the syllabus and teaching method are same across the country which is called "Central Schools" or Kendra Vidyalalyas, they all follow the textbooks written and published by NCERT, the CBSE has also affiliated schools in 21 other countries.

Similarly, another board was formed to replace the Cambridge School Certificate Examinations in 1956 which was run by the Inter-state Board for Anglo-Indian Education – (ISB-AIE) which is now called Indian Certificate of Secondary Education (CBSE) there are many schools affiliated to this board mostly private educational institutions set up by the colonial rulers and the Christians Churches catering to children from wealthy families. Then there a small number of schools who follow the Senior Cambridge curricula which are called ICSE

To improve the overall quality of education, the state governments introduced A Comprehensive and Continuous Evaluation (CCE) System to improve the overall personality development of the student instead of the dependence of single results of the final examinations. In states like Kerala Information

Technology as a subject was introduced at the high school level.

The new Education Policy of the Government of India enabled is the emphasis on Constructivism; IT enabled education, Free Software, and sharing educational resources. -
References:

Minute by the Hon'ble T B Macaulaly dated 2nd February 1835

Different types of Schooling in operation today.

Currently, there are 7 different types of school systems in operation today, teaching the same syllabus with common examinations conducted at the end of the year to assess the student's progress through grades and marks achieved.

Day scholars: The students attending in-person during the day at a fixed time of classes. There are government-run schools and also Private schools.

Boarding schools: Students studying in the designated school either with the day scholars at government school or private, with fixed time of classes or study in private boarding schools.

Night schooling: Where the students are either employed during the day or occupied otherwise, who attend in the evening school at a fixed time maybe 6.00pm to 10.00pm

Homeschooling: With the home school, parents become the teachers and provide students with personalized instruction customized to their own pace and learning style. Parents are subject to state rules to ensure students get a similar quality of education to what they would receive in the classrooms.

Distant education: With students learning from their home with the help of the syllabus provided, and learning through the help of guide books and write their exams at the designated school at the end of the term. These studies are for higher secondary and above classes.

Virtual Schooling: The schools that are conducted via the internet. Students usually take classes from the comfort of home and at their own pace. Follow the government syllabus and write their exams at centers approved by the Governments.

Special schools: The schools with children with disabilities who require special needs and attention to learning.

The schools, like the day scholars and boarding schools and Home Schooling all other schools, are mainly for their courses mainly for graduation and post-graduation studies, where there is no requirement of Labs & technical Workshops. Mostly, many of the other schools, besides the in-person classroom learning, progress, and the study is in the interest of the students, which is a huge drawback for the student's learning.

The studies are badly affected as there is no professional teaching staff who are specialized in these subject as teachers are professionally qualified, the teachers undergo professional courses for teaching us all the students' caliber is not the same in all of the schools. Therefore the method of conventional classroom schools is the most common and proven system, which is followed by all governments across the world.

The countries with the formal educations system in place have prospered and have grown economically, it is observed especially in Europe and Latin America, the advancement of education was at the peak in the 16thCentury, and their economy has grown at a rapid pace, with industrialization and innovation in products and services.

Most of today's progress in Literature, Science & technology, sports, and extracurricular activities are dominated these countries who are economically rich and developed nations, only in the last half-century, there is some progress in underdeveloped countries, due to stabilization of the economy, rapid changes in upgrading the knowledge and skills of the people, which was witnessed in these continents.

It is clearly evident in the world that with the emphasis on education, the economy in countries is rapidly growing, and the developments and uplift of the people are taking place at a much faster pace.

Now the question arises on how the poor economies will achieve this excellence in education at a much faster pace, and the answers to this are reformation in schooling with the method of adaptive modulation schooling, which will be detailed in the next chapters.

Science education in schools from class K-12:

In the teaching and learning of science to non-scientists, such as school children, college students, or adults within the general public, The field of science education includes in science content, science process (the science methods) some social science, and some teaching pedagogy, the standards for science education provide expectations for the development of understanding for students through the entire course of their K-12 education and beyond. The traditional subjects included in the standards and physical, life, earth space, and human science. India also follows the same pattern as the European model with slight changes under the central government NSD National skills development board preparing the students with the skills required to conform to those needed in that occupation at present.

Different Education Boards used by Governments and Private institutions.

Different boards are running the schools, like, Central Government-run schools, ISC, ICSC, and the state government or corporation run schools are SSC board, we also have international schools under IG board in some of the Public schools and Private schools.

Charter Schools: They are primary or secondary education institutions that do not charge a fee to the pupils who take state-mandated exams. These charter schools are subject to fewer rules, regulations, and statutes than the traditional state schools, but receive less public funding than the Government schools. These are non-profit charter schools. They follow the same syllabus of the state government schools, which are funded by the Local City Municipal Co-operations in Towns and Zilla Parishads schools in the villages.

Private & Public Schools: Which are wholly owned by Corporate bodies or Trusts, privately funded schools run mostly in cities which charge a fee to the pupil, based on the reputation of the schools and the facilities offered, there are also aided schools which are partially funded by the Trusts who are allowed to charge a nominal fee to the pupils. These schools can opt for either SSC board or ICS, IG board examinations. The students are admitted accordingly as per their choice of study.

Central Government schools: The federal government operates schools fully funded, there are other nominal charges taken from the children of the employees of the Central Government, those working in the Services, ARMY, Navy and Air-force personal and some of the Defense and Research Establishments, to facilitate their children's schooling, as and when there is a movement of the employees from the place of operations to another. Kendra Vidalia schools, Sainik Schools, and Institutional schools.

Most of the state Government or corporation run schools are lacking the facilities that are available in Public Schools, like filly operational Laboratories, with all equipment for their practice in the Science stream and Engineering, many of the schools are poorly furnished in Laboratories and Engineering technical workshops due to lack of funds allocated. Therefore many parents prefer to educate their children in private-public schools and colleges, who can afford, who are mostly living in big cities from an economically wealthy background.

There is a huge gap in the knowledge gap of the city students and the rural school students, the disparity between the student's knowledge, development, behavioral and social development, and their general knowledge are much lower standard compared to the Public schools or colleges, their ranks in the state or district level area are also not comparable to the students from the Public schools.

Therefore they develop an inferiority complex In the life of the student, his confidence level is down, his approach to life, his ambitions and vision are marred with negativism and the exposure to Sports and Games, outdoor activities are also restricted as the facilities and the encouragement is not supported with qualified teachers or the facilities in the schools whereby the students' growth is restricted.

Bridging the knowledge gap between Government and Private Public Schools.

The conventional method of teaching has to be changed and approach with a new method of education, imagination, determination, boldness, and urgency to facilitate the students with all the provisions that the private schools offer.

Allow the students to experience the adventure, freedom, and wonder of childhood with the practical guided training. To create an atmosphere conducive to the students learning, emphasizing the emotional and social behaviors of the child to excel and discover his potential in the interests of his choice and ability to perform.

Due to lack of facilities, the students are not blooming into the exceptional students that they can be, also due to the parental background and poverty. They are forced to perform the house choirs, where the students' development is restricted.

There is a great scoop for student learning in many poor countries run by the government schools by focusing on the change of the education system and give the right opportunities to the young children, starting with primary and secondary education, with a good enrolment of students in higher education, which will ultimately be the driving force for the growth of the economy of any country.

All children have the right to high-quality education.

Don't miss the chance to move your classroom, school, or district forward by creating a cultural shift and following through with the school-wide and classroom practices that have been tested by educators. It is the right of all citizens to be educated free up to the age of 16 years.

Therefore to bridge this gap, we have to reform our schooling systems, which is conducive to the current circumstances and also utilize the modern technology available for easy communication and interacting with distant places with ease and utilizing the infrastructure for all school students.

Teachers Remuneration and Assessments.

The teaching professionalism is a vital element for the survival of any economy of any country. The salary of a teacher depends on various factors such as years of experience, location, private schools or government-funded education, additional qualifications, etc. Generally, higher / secondary school teachers earn a higher income than elementary school teachers.

The salary range in most of the developed countries ranges from $110000/- to lower $65000/- and most of the Asian countries, the average salary is about USD$3564/- in government and private schools. Still, the incentives for working in rural areas in Australia will earn you an additional to $20,000 incentive annually and also rent re-embarrassment of up to 90% in different schools, where the teacher will to go to rural areas to teach in schools. There are no such incentives for our teachers In India. Therefore the quality of teaching is very poor and teachers with mostly no professional qualifications to teach In schools.

Part III:

Formal Education System prevailing in the World.

The Education system which is prevalent in the world since 16th to 21st Century in many countries is as follows:

Education in the United Kingdom and the European countries:

The education system in the UK is divided into four main parts, Primary education, secondary education, and higher education, which runs from about 5 years old until the student is 16 years old. Generally, it is a primary school and secondary school.

The Government has made it compulsory for all children in the Primary education from the year 1880 funded by the Government, and there is an enrollment of 99% children in the primary section, all are subject to assessment and inspection by the Office for Standards in Education Children's Services and Skills- (OSECSS)

The early year's foundation schools, which are pre-primary and kindergarten schools below 3 and 4 years old, are also funded by the governments.

At the end of year 15 or 16 years, the students typically take their (GCSE) General Certificate of Secondary Education, who want to pursue academic qualifications until end of 13 years of schooling or 18years of age, which is equivalent to high schools examinations in other countries, the UK students must complete before planning to go to college or university.

Education in Scotland: has its own education system, on them in (GIRFEC) Getting It Right For Every Child, is a national approach to improving the wellbeing of the children and young people, with the inputs of "Put the best interests of the child at the heart of every decision making.)

Enhancing Learning and teaching through the use of Digital Technology – A digital learning and teaching strategy for Scotland. The objective is to ensure that digital technology is a central consideration in all areas of curriculum and assessment delivery.

Education in Scotland has also set up 'Upstream-Protecting the next child" It is an online resource that enables adults in Scotland to prevent child sexual abuse and to protect the next child.

The system of education has evolved into ongoing changes to bring about excellence in the learners. One of the most prominent is the Early Learning and Childcare, which is followed in most of the countries.

ELS- is the generic term for the full range of early learning and childcare provision, including family centers, nursery schools, nursery classes, and attended to primary schools and childminders.

Professional learning is key to the effectiveness of all those who work in early learning and childcare.

All who wish to teach must hold a Teacher Qualification (TQ) and pass the mandatory Government teachers qualification test (GTQT) for all early education and K-12

Luxembourg schooling

There are also specialized schools for Sports, Languages, Adult Education and Post –Primary (All those who have not completed the primary level of education) though the Trilingualisim is featured heavily in Luxembourgish preschool levels onwards, French in the primary and German in the secondary schools while additional languages such as Spanish, Italian and Latin are available at the same level, the University level, English is used frequently.

During all levels of pre-university levels education, at least 50% of the hours are used for teaching languages.

Most of the European schools follow the same pattern of education in schools and Universities, the standard is very high. The assessments are very stringent, but modern education has more emphasis on the Languages.

Education System in Australia:

The Australian system of education mandates compulsory education of all children up to the age of 16 Years.

The Australian Qualifications Framework(AQF) is the policy for regulated qualifications in the Australian education and training system. The AQF was introduced in 1995. The key objectives of the Australian Qualifications Framework are to facilitate pathways to and through formal qualifications. The education of all government schools in 2019 were 65.7% enrolled in the governments' schools, 19.7 % in catholic schools and 14.6%, and the rest in independent schools in Australia. Of the total population and of which 40 % study in non –governmental schools. The budget for 2019 was 5.9% of the GDP. University education is very robust and is the third-largest provider for university education after UAS. The UK followed by Canada.

Education in the United States of America:

Larry Summers, At the time President of Harvard University concurred. "He said, one of the key problems with K-12education in America is that education schools push out the notion that a kid needs self-esteem to achieve. But it is the other way around the kid needs to achieve in order to build self-esteem."

Education is provided in public, private, and home schools. State governments set overall educational standards, often mandate standardized tests for K-12, public school systems and supervise, usually through a board of regents, state colleges, and universities. The student enrolled in schools in America in the year 2019. Primary: 37.9 Million

Secondary: 26.1 Million

Post-secondary 20.5 Million

Secondary diploma: 91%

Post-secondary diploma: 46%

Reference: *National center for education statistics (NCES)*

Colonial-era to 19th Century: In the year 1639, Harvard College established, and then in 1853, Protestants and Catholics opened over hundreds of small denominational colleges in the 19th Century and enrolled 46% of all US undergraduates.

To handle the explosive growth of K-12 education, every state set up a network of teachers, colleges, beginning with Massachusetts in 1830, later they became state colleges and then state universities with board curriculum.

Junior college grew from 20 in number in 1909 to 137, rapid expansion continued in 1920 with 400 Junior colleges and enrolled 70,000 students.

The 20th century saw a slow growth with about 1000 colleges and students of 1,60,000. In the mid 20th century, state universities grew from small institutions of fewer than 1000 students to campuses with 40,000 or more students, with networks of regional campuses around the state, in turn, regional campuses broke away and became separate universities.

This brought about exponential growth in the Education system, and many students benefited as it became affordable. As competition built up, the common man had the opportunity to be educated and improve his standard of living.

Developing the Education Profession. (DEP):With the backdrop of the objectives of working with a range of national partners and with practitioners to ensure that professional development is effective and impacts positively on the outcome for all learners.

The American Federation of Teachers (AFT): 875000 T researched various industrialized countries and chose for its series to Define world-class standards, those countries where the standards for students were the most rigorous. It is found that Japan is among the most challenging tests given to students in these countries and is required for all college-bound students.

The United States has no official national exams, nor does it have anyway, privately administered exams taken by a large number of students nationwide. The SAT and ACT are the most widely taken exams, are designed mainly for college-bound students. Which assesses only a very narrow range of skills and knowledge?

The (GED) exams are taken by students in school by adults wishing to obtain a high school equivalency degree.

It vibes neither the teacher nor the students an appropriate measure of and incentive for realistically high achievements, which deludes students to believing a high grade represents real high achievement. US schools are concentrating too much on preparing youngsters for college and ignoring students who will be seeking jobs in a rapidly changing world.

Their performance in school and colleges and the options that have will be available to them after they complete their compulsory education. There is a systematic mechanism in place for moving young people into the workforce with the appropriate skills as well as a good foundation for all later learning, whether it is academic or vocational.

Education in African Countries:

Of all regions, sub-Saharan Africa has the highest rate of education exclusion. Over one-fifth of children between the ages of 6-11years are out of school, followed by one-third of youth between the ages of about 12-14 years old.

Without urgent action, the situation will likely get worse as the region faces a rising demand for education due to the still-growing school-age population. -UNESCO-UIS.

There are 10 countries joining the CapED initiative with the UIS and UNESCO efforts to help build the gap between national education policies and data collection and use.

In particular, the UIS is supporting countries to develop their own action plans to improve the quality and use of their data to track progress towards the Sustainable Development Goal for quality education for all by 2030 at the national level. This will also directly contribute to improving the reporting of internationally comparable data.

The countries must fix their education urgently, starting from their early schooling and simultaneously work on the higher education system.

Education in Asian countries:

Indonesia:

The 4th most populated country struggles to provide inclusive, high-quality education to its citizens; the country has much lower literacy levels than those of other Southeast Asian nations. The percentage of Indonesians over the age of 25 that attained at least a bachelor's degree in 2016 was just under 9% lowest of all the member states of ASEAN.

According to the data from the UNESCO Institute of Statistics- UIS, the tertiary, gross enrollment ratio (GER) leaped by 20 % in 2004 -2017, despite being low overall. It now compares with other countries at 36.5% compared with 28.3% in Vietnam, 42% in Malaysia, and 49.3% Thailand – (UIS). And their percentage of GDP has stagnated over the past decade and remains well below recommended levels for emerging economics at 3.6% much lower than most of the ASEAN region nations.

The Educational system is supportive of the common people, 24% of the population still live in poverty, and more than half that live in extreme poverty. The youth unemployment has doubled from 2000 -2017 the ILO has recently noted that 27% of the youths aged 15-24 are not engaged in any form of education, employment or training in 2018.

With the National Education Policy: Tremendous progress has been made in these areas over the past decade, the net enrollment ratio in elementarily education, for instance, now stands at more than 90% compared to 60% in the mid-1980 UNESCO Data, the adult literacy rate likewise, surged from 35% to 73% in 2017. Even today, many classrooms are overcrowded, and teaches are often poorly trained, and the teacher-student ration also being very low. Dropout rates are high, with nearly 20% of pupils not completing elementary school in 2016. At the lower secondary level, the dropout rate stood at 38% in 2017, with fully 42% of girls leaving school before completing grade 10, due to factors like poverty and child marriage. The teacher-to-student ratio is well above the official target ratio of 30:1 a 42:1 in secondary schools -2016

The introduction of national examinations at the elementary level mushroomed private tutoring industry and placing children from low-income households are a disadvantage since their parents are unable to afford such services. Private tutoring is a lucrative and growing business in Bangladesh. According to UNESCO, more than half of all secondary students in the country use private tutors. The has savior shortage in tertiary, gross enrollment ratio (GER) thought it is 7% higher but much lower by 10% compared to INDIA, there is a huge shortage in the Infrastructure In colleges and Universities with and relied primarily on the part-time teaching staff. Similar are the problems in most of the ASEAN countries.

The Education System in China:

The Chinese schooling system is one of the robust and offers perceived as a breeding ground for highly educated future professionals. The metropolises seem to offer great quality education and, in the rural area, aren't as developed. They are often terribly understaffed, and the student's opportunities and education environment are radically different from those in the big cities.

The National exams are high pressure, many students burn out, and stories of depression and suicide are not unheard of. The Primary state schools are funded by the government and charge nominal charges for food and other activities.

High schools, colleges, and universities in china usually have their own grading system. The main difference between public and private education in china is that private schools tend to use bilingual teaching.

The Chinese school curriculum typically has very strict rules, the emphasis of discipline, endless homework and tests, and constant pressure from peers and teachers-that seems to be the daily life of a Chinese student.

The primary schools have the Chinese language and math as the big two. Additionally, children are instructed in music, art, morals, and society and nature and also practical's work classes and additional extra-curricular activities to the mix. In fact, the competitiveness of the educational system in china starts very early on, so parents often sign their kids up to a variety of extracurricular activities in order for them to have better prospects in the future.

Whatever they choose to continue their education after middle schooling, the students have to take ZHONGKAO-senior high school entrance examination.

The GAOKAO (National Higher Education Entrance Examination) test is the toughest high school graduation exam. The main goal is to prepare the students for higher educations. The 9 hrs exam that Is taken 3 days is a grueling test, and only 40 % of the first-timers pass and all are admitted to the universities.

Education System in Bangladesh.

 All citizens must undertake twelve years of compulsory education which consists of eight years in primary school level and four years at high school level, both the education is financed by the state and free of charges in all public schools. The GPD spend on the education has been very low, just a 2.20 % of the GDP, however with their meager funds they have yet been able to achieve a good education results because of their stringing implementation policies.

The-primary education is of 7 years starting from pre-primary to 5 the standard; the change has brought in many more children into the education system.

PART IV:

Factors affecting performances in low economies.

Lack of political will and the low priority given in the budgets has affected the education system with poor infrastructure and Teacher-student ration being very low s affecting student's performance. Primarily there are schools run by Governments of the states with the Central government advice; the education system is built upon in most of the countries with different boards in place to operate schools with the different board curriculum and syllabus in place, there are different boards in a place like CBSC, SSC, ICSC, and ISC. There are also international Baccalaureate (IB) and Cambridge International Examinations (CIB). The International curriculum and exams are conducted by the universities or governments, depending on which country it is.

There are many schools already moving to Blended learning in many countries. Fresh teaching practices with technological inputs of Online teaching, helping to create a rewarding classroom environment and in-person classrooms blending both to given an environment for the teachers, Leaders, and Learners, involving multiple stakeholders providing education with innovative ideas.

In countries like America, Europe, and Australia the Blended learning Schools are in rapid progress in many schools and colleges due to the Covid-19, Pandemic and the lockdown imposed by many governments, in the process many students in the charter schools and some private school students do not have access to the technology. These students are at a disadvantage compared to others.

Socio-Economic Factors affecting education.

Some of the countries which have established the formal education, much earlier than the Asian and African countries, like Western European countries, United Kingdom, USA, have grown economically very strong, compared to the Asian and African continents, had their Schools, Colleges and Universities were well established in the 1500 and 1600 centuries.

This education has churned out a large number of highly educated students who could bring in Industrial revolution in these countries which propelled their economy to very high levels and the whole balance of power shifted to Europe who had ruled 3/4th of the world with money, the invention of new products and military might.

The rise of Asian Countries:

With the formation of the United Nations, after World War-II, there was more democracy in the countries, and this established a central elected power governing the country and formulation of the constitution and the rule of law.

Many countries established schools and colleges in the model of the education system of the United Kingdom model of schools and colleges, which are now prevalent in the current system of education.

Since the poor economies and unstable governments in many African countries have affected the education of the children and due to lack of government policies and implementation, the education performance of the citizens has failed to achieve any significant growth.

PART V:

Industrialization and Natural disasters, effecting the Education of the students in the World.

With the fast industrial developments in many countries especially countries like USA, Russia, China, Europe, and the Middle Eastern countries, with the migration of people from different countries and from their own small villages, towns, moved into cities, pushed up the requirements for infrastructures for education and has put a great burden on the Civic bodies.

There are drastic changes in the ecology, and we have all are susceptible to floods, Suami, plagues, earthquakes, and pandemics, has changed the world, the cities in many countries becoming large industrial and economic hubs, the villages and towns neglected, with industrial development in the cities, the economic disparity between the towns and cities and the affordability of schooling has become very expensive in private schools. Government schools have no standard of education compared to their peers in the cities.

Lack of need to adapt to changes in the World is slowing the economy.

Less than half of public school students have been White. The percentage of public school students who are White is projected to continue to decline through at least fall 2028, along with the percentages of students who are Pacific Islander and American Indian/ Alaska Native. The percentage of students who are Hispanic, Asian, and two or more races is projected to increase in the coming years. The black students are expected to be about the same in 2028.

There are 70 % of the American people who have not gone to college, similar is the statistics in European countries, and the Colleges are filled with the students from underdeveloped and poor countries the statistics indicate there are 12.1 million students currently studying in USA full-time courses. There are 1197000 international students studying in the USA every year from different countries like China have 397000 students and India with 203000 who are majorly dominating in higher education besides countries like South Korea, Saudi Arabia, and Canada. In all, there are huge revenues in the education industry in the developed countries, who had established their education system. Now it is a $40.0Billion business in America besides there are other major destinations for the international students like UK, Australia and Canada for higher education, neglecting their on education in rural areas and small towns, not bringing about the reforms required in these areas impacting a generation of citizens and stagnated economies.

Today most of the service Industries in Information Technology, Hospitals, Doctors, and Engineers are Chinese and Indians origin in America, and since the Indian's have the advantage of English speaking besides the focus on Engineering, they have dominated in all technological Industries. Similarly, most of the manufacturing products in the world are supplied from China, which is now the fastest-growing economy in the world.

(NCES)indicates that in America there were 56.6 million students attend elementary, middle, and high schools across the US of these 50.8 million students in public schools and 5.8.million in private schools and of which again 6.1million attend Pre-kindergarten and kindergarten, 35.3 million attend pre-kindergarten to grade, 8th, 15.3million attend grade 9-12 and 4.1 million attend 9th grade to high school, and 3.7 million students graduate from high school and surprisingly 3.3million pass from public schools and 03 million from private schools.

Countries like Japan and many European countries who were well advanced in Manufacturing and military power have failed to capitalize on their strengths as they have not undertaken any reforms in their education system at the primary level and Higher secondary to educate their children for future job competency, whereby stagnating their economy as the children are not future-ready.

Though most of these developed countries had well-established schools and colleges, universities and research center their outlook and approach towards the changing world, and fast technological developments in many countries, the people are moving to different cities and different countries, the requirements are changing, countries who can adapt to the changes and educate their children will now dominate, countries like Japan, Russia, and Western European countries who are not adapting to the change, of Language, Engineering, technology and Science, the needs as per the Global demands will drift backward, the economy of these countries either stagnant or sliding to negative growth all these countries cannot adapt to the change.

PART-VI:

Reformations is continues process adapting to the changing requirements.

Adapt Education to the needs of the World.

Build systems to educate the students to learn to the changing technology in the world and adapting to the effects of Natural disasters and Pandemics.

Those countries who can educate the next generation with high standards, imparting high-quality knowledge to all the students in cities and rural areas will dominate the World and now is the time for especially, nations like India and China with students aspiring to study in many well-established colleges and universities is prominently visible across the world, today the students from these countries are studying in highly rated universities all across the globe acquiring knowledge and skill required for the current times.

But the transformation of schooling must come from the grass route levels, which are Primary and Secondary schooling, which will uplift the countries from poverty and propel them to become superpowers.

Alternative methods of teaching.

Adaptive Schooling Modulation System can revive the failing schooling module, which is now not relevant to the fast growth of Technology and Artificial Intelligence. The current system of education has become irrelevant.

Having schools specialized for teaching different subjects and build infrastructure and teaching methods suitable to impart the best.

Use technology to maximize the number of students in different parts of the region to be educated with the best standards prevailing in cities.

Build Core schools to train the students in Experiential Learning, Transformational Learning, Experimental Learning, Instructional Learning, like extra-curricular activities, Physical exercises, Sports, and Games with the best of the equipment to excel in each of these activities.

This will completely eliminate the disparity in the education of the students and will build a competitive environment in the schools. Governments, Education leaders, Administrators must support the change in the education systems:

Governments must approach with imagination, determination boldness, and urgency to transform schooling systems across the globe so as not to fail the people of the nations, an option for better opportunities in life.

State governments and the boards of education must, in conjunction with the central government's policies, execute reforms in schools, and there will be a new generation of students well equipped to bring about the change in the next 20 Years.

The seeds are plenty in Asia, Africa, and China, it is to be sown on good ground, and it will yield in plentiful in the next 20 Years.

Reformation of schooling must start from basic units in society, the individuals, Governments, Leaders and school boards, and the private partners for a successful implementation in reforming the school educations.

Transition and building Alliances with different partners in the field of education:

The transition in these phases of the working atmosphere is a challenge to many schools that have been operating in conventional schooling for centuries, which was brought to us from the colonial rule countries, whose system of education was relevant in those days. It now requires the cooperation of all the stakeholders in the education system to make it operational, the Governments of the day, school Boards, Leaders, School administrators, Principals, and Private partners to execute the new schooling structure.

We see this, In the case of Hotels, Hospitals and now many other Enterprises in the World like UBAR, OYO, WEWORK, UPWORK, and many such organizations working globally, as we see in the case of hotels, the builder, builds as per the requirement of the hotel. The Operator is the one who runs the business. Similarly, we can have Private players who can build the infrastructure facilities as required, if it is a Laboratory or Botanical Gardens, Animal Farm, or Engineering Workshops, and the schools to be utilized for In-Person classroom teaching with all the modern infrastructure and amenities.

Build facilities and infrastructure for effective collaboration, teamwork, and networking in schools.

In-person classroom schools which will teach only subjects which are theoretical in nature, Philosophy Languages, History, etc., for revisions for subjects and on one-to-one interaction with the teacher - students who are mainly not able to cope up, and the their studies.

Online teaching will again emphasize on teaching through multimedia from remote locations, the objective is to cover a large number of students at the same time.

Similarly schools with the facilities like Laboratories, Workshops, Botanical gardens, Zoological facilities specifically for teaching purpose for the students in this field of studies.

Schools for all outdoor activities, like Games, Sports, Drill, Yoga, all physical activities, where their best facilities are provided for the use of all schools in that region continuously.

Auditoriums and Theaters for the students in Arts, fine arts, and music to learn, practice, and perform, with modern facilities for the exclusive use of the students of all schools under the region or circle of operation.

The new system proposal of educations will give all the schools in Public, Private, or Government school students' equal opportunity of learning with the best facilities to excel in their field of interest.

Enhancing learning through the use of digital technology. -

Digital learning: Curricula for Excellence: (CfE) It is instructed around 4 key areas, the skills of the educators, access to technology, curriculum and assessment, and the leadership.

This statement is intended to provide clear, practical advice for teachers and practitioners on planning learning, teaching, and assessment. Teachers should be empowered to use the flexibility that CfE provides to organize learning for children and young people in the way best suits and meets the needs.

Acellus Academy high school, Kansas City, Missouri. The USA.

Acellus Is an International Science Academy, teaching online classes for K-12 in 4200 Public Schools. As a distance education school, Acellus Academy serves a diverse population of students located throughout the United States.

Acellus Academy provides instruction online through distance education via the Acellus Learning System that has been used to provide primary instruction to millions of students in thousands of schools throughout the United States.

The online curriculum is taught by Master Teachers from across the nation that has been recognized for their expertise in both content material and conveying knowledge through video instruction.

Students who enroll are typically looking for an alternative to traditional school settings for a variety of reasons, such as a medical necessity, interest In more rigorous coursework, safety from bullying issues, a flexible learning environment and independent studies for students who have dropped out of school and need a second chance for success, improving student achievement, specifically in the area of math and science education.

Families meet their student's needs through online schooling, for those studying in Home Schooling, Special schools, children with medical issues who cannot attend schools, students who are pursuing fields like Sports, a study inconvenient timings.

Infrastructure resources and transitioning of school teaching.

The new system of education will facilitate teaching staff to be highly skilled in their respective subjects of learning, be it theory, practical or outdoor activities.

The schools will employ highly trained staff for teaching in their respective field of operations like Laboratory, Engineering, Art, and Music, which will include support staff.

The schools with the above facilities will operate as an independent profit center in guidance with the Government rules and regulations.

Principals and Practices of collaborative Rolls and Responsibilities:

The schools with In-person teaching will primarily be taking admissions of the students. They will be overall responsible for the progress of the studies of each student, the syllabus will be completed as per the guidelines of the Governments or boards and conduct examinations on the system currently prevailing in schools, the students will be promoted based on the results declared.

The revenue will be shared with the different schools providing the facilities to the students, on the school to school basis, which is fixed by the Government / Boards.

The curriculum for the students must be compulsorily completed with their Practical as required in a different specialized school for writing their board exams.

Building alliances with Governments and Private Universities in the world:

It gives teachers, administrators, and every member of the transition team practical tools to facilitate collaboration, empowering all participants to utilize the infrastructure and improve post-school outcomes.

The governments are benefited in terms of Costs of setting up schools with complete facilities, recruiting qualified teachers in rural areas, and maintaining the infrastructure.

The teachers get the satisfaction of imparting their knowledge adequately and be proud of their prodigies.

The students get the full knowledge equally, be it in rural areas or city schools, either Private Public Schools or Government-run local schools, they can continue in pursuit of higher education or sports and excel in all their activities.

In the next 20 Years, with adaptive school modulation system of education in place, there will be great progress and development of nations, in all aspects of life will improve with new Innovations, Technological Developments, Artificial Intelligence. The Economy will take a giant leap and making all the countries self-reliant and give their citizens a better standard of life, the disparity between the poor and the rich countries will be narrowed down.

Operations of the schools in the new Adaptive Modulation Schooling must be clearly defined in terms of the school curriculum.

PART VII:

REFORMATIONS IN SCHOOLING IN INDIA:

"Schools by fostering student-centered learning, and accountable, blueprint for change involves other elements, to such as technology transformation, distance learning, engagement of parents and the participation of philanthropists and other members of the private sector."- - Joel Klein.

STEPS OF REFORMATIONS:

Adaptive Modulation School Method 01

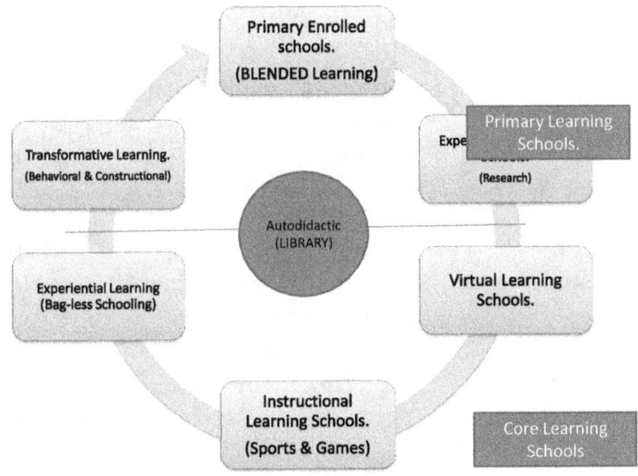

1. **Blended Learning Schools**: In-person and Online teaching, for better utilization of existing infrastructure in Schools, they should convert all schools into core study schooling for specific learning or activities. All infrastructures built for the modern education system should facilitate (Sharing of schools for Learning and Research work.)with the existing resources.

2. **Experimental Learning** schools will facilities for Laboratories and Engineering Workshops, other schools like Experiential Learning Schools with Botanical Gardens, Zoo & Animal farms, Museums & Art Galleries (NEP refers to these schools as **Bag-Less Learning**) on shared learning basis with all nearby schools.

Experimental Learning Schools

Botany.	Zoology.	Physics.	Chemistry.
Lab Experiments.	Lab Experiments.	Lab Experiments.	Lab Experiments.
Visit Gardens.	Visit Zoo.	Introduction to AI	Visit Pharmacy Co.
Participate in Shows	Animal Farms, Bird	Participate in Tech	

Experimental Learning in Schools-02

3. **Instructional Learning schools**, like Theaters, Auditoriums, Aquariums, Stadiums, Swimming pools, Play Grounds to be put into use for teaching specifically the stream the student's interest to learn and excel, at different levels of education from primary to the Universities level, which must be part of their curriculum.

The governments benefit due to the utilization of existing infrastructure and each unit becoming self-sustainable and revenue generation, the private sector also can participate In such CORE schools, such as animal farms, Aquariums, Swimming pools, Botanical Gardens, Zoo, which are currently run in Australia and other countries by private firms, the infrastructure can be utilized by both, the general public and also all teaching schools.

This helps the Administrators and the Educators, the burden of budgets, the resources can be utilized to the maximum, the students are benefited to do live experiential learning and field study.

Stadiums.	Play Grounds.	Gymnastics.	Swimming Pools.	Disciplinary activities.
Athletics and other competitive games.	Cricket. Football. Tennis courts. Basket ball. Hockey and many others.	Apparatus, Floor exercises. Vault and Long Horse.	Synchronized diving. Competitive swimming.	National cadet corps. Scouts and Guides.

•All the Games and sports activities must be nurtured at the early age of a child, from primary schooling onwards, especially Gymnastics, the flexibility and movements are easily adaptable. The interest in all sports activities of a child are identified and guided to excel in each of the fields.
•Some of the schools in Russia and Western European countries start at early schooling.

<u>Instructional Scaffolding Learning-03</u>

Community learning Schools and Colleges:

These community schools/colleges are spread over and the land of 150 to 300 Acers campus, housing the departments of the college, which includes Classrooms, Research Laboratories, Technical Workshops, Central Library, Auditoriums, Playgrounds, Swimming pools, Gymnasiums and Living quarters for students, faculty & support staff

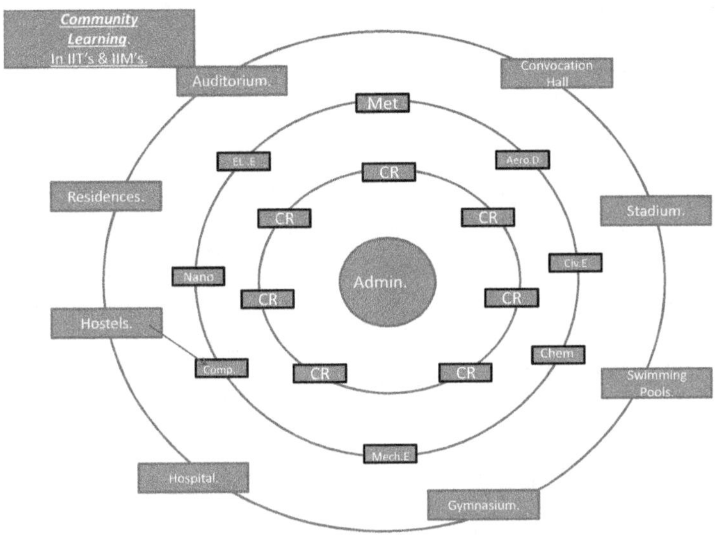

COMMUNITY LEARNINT SCHOOLS-04

The Community colleges are similar to a University Education, sharing all the Common facilities in the campus yet pursuing their core stream of studies, which have found to produce exceptional results than the standalone colleges of the same stream since the facilities are shared the budget is minimal. The facilities are much higher standard compared to standalone colleges, where the budgets don't permit.

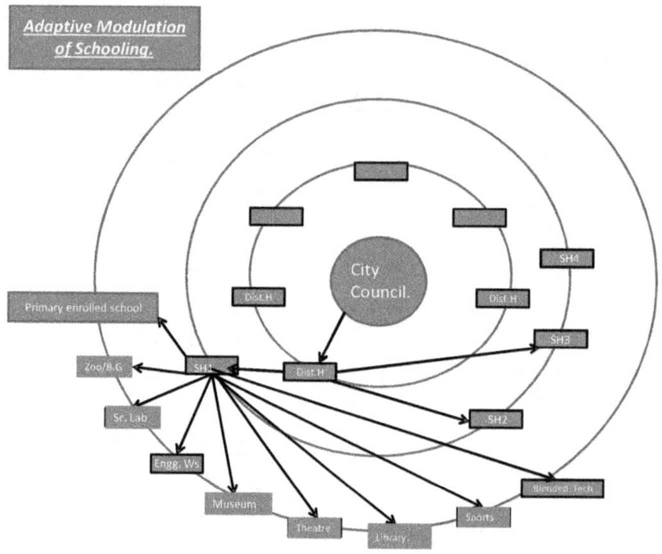

<u>NEW Adaptive Modulation -05</u>

Similarly, The Adaptive modulation of schooling will have the same effect when all the facilities are shared as community education in the town or city by all the schools.

The infrastructure costs are shared by all the schools in that in the nearby areas.

The facilities are utilized by all the students in that area, unlike now with uneven substandard facilities or no facilities, compared to many of the Private Public Schools and colleges, this system will allow better usage of resources.

The student's enthusiasm in studies is unbound with the new system to perform, and to excel in assessments and make his dream achievable.

It gives equal opportunities to every student, be it rural or urban schools and colleges.

The standard of education provided is the same for Government-run, and Private operated colleges and schools across the region.

The competition between the Schools and Colleges can still be healthy in terms of other facilities, such as Air-conditioned classrooms, College or School security and other peripheral facilities, Hostel, Food, Transport, etc. offered by the primary enrolled School or Colleges.

The advantage for the School / College management is, the facilities are used to the optimum level, including the teaching staff and generating additional revenue from those schools and colleges utilizing their facilities. It is a win-win situation for both the schools/colleges,

It raises the standards of education for those who are hiring the best facilities also use their funds for more useful academic needs.

Non-collegiate education.

Non- Collegiate education: **Non-collegiate women's education board (NCWEB)** was established in the year 1943, by the Delhi University, it enables women students to take some of the examinations of the university with special coaching but without attending regular classes. Today it has an enrollment of more than 24,000 students. But the condition is that only students residing in the national capital territory of Delhi are allowed to enroll.

The major advantage of the NON-Collegiate programmers of teaching is its low cost and utilization of the existing infrastructure of educational institutions during Saturday /Sunday and academic breaks.

This system of education must be extended to both Men and Women in different cities, to upgrade their learning skills both in rural and urban education centers.

Under the UNDP and NSDC (University of Delhi) Collegiate comprises of different collages (The Oxford collegiate system) which is part of a University, the government must mandate for compulsory employment in Industries of at least 10 % of the students for skills development with incentives to industry and stipend paid to students.

Blended Learning Schools:

"Whether you are a district, school, or classroom education leader, Blended Learning in Action will take you through pedagogy, tools, curriculum, and lesson design strategies, and practical classroom models to start transforming learning for your students. Blended learning has to provide educators with innovative ideas whether they are just considering going blended, read to take the plunge, or have already gone blended and are looking for more inspiration Don't miss the chance to move classroom, school, or district forward you creating a culture shift and following through with the school-wide and classroom practices that have been tested by educators" – **Kerry Gallagher, Digital Learning Specialist- K-12**

Human Insights.

people

Skills with

How we Learn.

Through sight.	83%
Through hearing.	11%
Through smell.	3 ½%
Through Touch.	1 ½%
Through Taste.	1%
-	-

How we retain information.

Of what we read.	10%
Of what we hear.	20%
Of what we see.	30%
Of what we see and hear.	50%
Of what we say as we talk.	70%
What we say as we do a thing.	90%

<u>## Human Insights-1-06</u>

The MOOC is a Massive Open Online Course aimed at unlimited participation and open access via the web. It became popular in 2010-14 in addition to traditional course materials such as filmed lectures, readings and problem sets, many MOOC's provide interaction between students, professors, and teaching assistants. But with Blended teaching with the modern technology available, the teaching is more practical, informative, interactive, and problem-solving. The students can interact with their peers and teacher in a virtual class as in-person classes. This gives the advantages of the student to learn from anywhere.

<u>Human Insight.</u>

Method of Instructions.	Recall 3 hours later.	Recall 3 days later.
Telling when used alone.	70%	10%
Showing when used alone.	72%	20%
When a blend of telling and showing is used.	85%	65%

<u>## Human Insight-2-07</u>

<u>eVidya (E-Learning)</u>

<u>Visual Learning-08</u>

Visual Learning through technology and mass learning in schools has many benefits, The visual learning has a lasting and retraceable impact on the students' education, the process is very simple which can be transmitted through a media center by qualified teachers in the subject and given equal learning opportunities with the same standard for many schools simultaneously.

You can incorporate, as shown in the chart very easily, bringing in many examples from across the world.

Student's assessments and grading:

People usually confuse assessment and grading to be the same thing, although these terms are connected closely, they are still very different from each other.

Grading is a method of evaluating a student's performance; it is done in the form of percentages, marks, .Grades are usually given on activities like projects, assignments, tests, and more.

Like behavior, attendance, participation, helplessness, teachers grade them accordingly in the respective fields.

Whereas assessment is all about evaluating those grades, to assess a student's performance, the teacher needs some data. That data comes in the form of grades, from blended learning schools.

Formative assessment: A range of formal and informal assessment procedures conducted by teachers during the learning process. For example, a student getting grade 'C' in science is grading, but realizing the problems as to why he/she is getting grade 'C' is assessment. Most importantly, grades assign students with actual objectives to achieve, and assessment comes with benefits of its own it assists in classifying the weak zones of a student.

The assessment allows for two-way interactions, It involves the student as much as the teacher, it focuses more on the student rather than the technicalities of teaching.

Grades are useful for organizations to measures student's performance, and assessment is useful for teachers to give them an insight into the student's progress. That is to say, both have equal importance; they can be used appropriately wherever the need arises. In short, grading is beneficial in assessing large data, whereas assessment works for assessing individual data.

The pedagogy with regards to student learning is of utmost importance for the holistic growth and knowledge of a child. In today's teaching methods are mostly textbook knowledge, which is restricting the child's thinking ability and applying to the practical situation.

The teachers must be redrawn into new pedagogical methods of teaching from K-12, which in the long run, will change the approach of the students learning as he proceeds to the higher schooling or colleges.

Let us look at what is the study of pedagogy.

Transformative Learning Schools:

Pedagogy: Most commonly understood as the approach to teaching refers to the theory and practice of learning and how this process influences and is influenced by the social, political, and psychological development of learners.

Pedagogy, taken as an academic discipline, is the study of how knowledge and skills are imparted in an educational context, and it considers the interactions that take place during learning both the theory and practices of pedagogy vary greatly, as they reflect different social political and cultural contexts.

Pedagogy is often described as the act of teaching; The pedagogy adopted by the teachers shape their actions, judgments strategies by taking into consideration theories of learning, understandings of students and their needs, and the backgrounds and interests of individual students. Its aims may range from furthering

liberal education (the general development of human potential) to the narrower specifics of vocational education (Imparting and acquisition of specific skills). Conventional western pedagogic views the teacher as a knowledge holder and the student as the recipient of knowledge, but theories of pedagogy increasingly identify the student as an agent and the teacher as a facilitator.

Instructive strategies are governed by the pupil's background knowledge and experience, situation, and environment, as well as learning goals set by the student and teacher. One example would be the Socratic Method. Reference: Wikipedia.org.

PRE- SCHOOLING IN INDIAN STATE- RUN DAYCARE CENTRES. (ANGANWADI CENTERS.)

The Integrated Child Development Services (ICDS) programmer who provides food and primary healthcare to children less than six years of age and their mothers at these Anganwadi or Day Care centers.

The Anganwadi workers primarily are for distribution of provision of food to children and lactating mothers, and about 27 Lakhs of them at 14 Lakhs center's across the country are working in the Ministry of Women and Child Development.

The government is now shifting the emphasis to convert Anganwadi into the center of pre-school education. As a result, a massive exercise is being launched to Train the

Anganwadi workers to become pre-school teachers, as per the ministry of WCD- Ref: NDTV Education

The early learning of the child up to the age of 6 years should be of prime importance as all the future learning of the students in based on early learning and development of the brain of the child. This will have a strong bearing on the child's influence in the development and learning skills and cannot be left the Anganwadi.

The idea of the WDC to convert all Anganwadi centers into Pre-primary schools is the right approach for the development and in the early learning of a child.

 "The clay has to be molded into a beautiful shape, and then it can be painted to different shades to beautify."

The better method of teaching would be to employ professionally trained teachers with early learning-teaching skills, which creates a desire among the students to move upwards to primary and secondary schooling.

The lactating mothers who are in the scheme must also be trained in skills like tailoring, handicraft, and other life-supporting skills.

The process will benefit the prenatal supportive role in the development of the child's education.

Creating a Learning environment- Anganwadi

It is strongly proposed to have qualified teachers in each Anganwadi center and have basic tools to teach the pre-primary schools and use Online classes broadcasting to hundreds of schools at the school timings and take the assistance of the Schoolteacher posted at each center, to guide the students and the Anganwadi workers. They, in turn, can impart lessons based on broadcasting to the children.

Digital teaching In Anganwadi centers:

The advantage of the Online teaching at the center is that it can display many pictures on the screen, show different animals, Birds, play toys, learn alphabets and simple counting, language, to form a sentence to speak and play rimes, Dance and make many more physical activities.

Spotlight on new tools and method of teaching, especially through Multimedia:

This method will give a professional approach to the learning and inculcate discipline in the students and Anganwadi workers. A formal method of teaching in

schools will be inculcated among the children, who will have a great advancement in their primary schooling.

The government's emphasis is more on higher secondary schooling. There is not much of e-learning in the lower classes, especially in the Pre-school curriculum. Where the need is the most, the students can grasp on visual learning faster as they are not trained to read and write.

AI in Anganwadi - Pre- School Leanings:

There is also a strong suggestion for the use of Artificial Intelligence in these Anganwadi Centers – or Pre-schools, for learning the basics, which are programmed with the software installed to perform the necessary tasks as required, the whole emphasis is to impart knowledge in the correct and best suitable method of learning to the students in mass education.

Early development of a child's mental and physical growth and healthy child is essential for the future wellbeing of the family.

This will also help facilitate implementing many schemes of the Government easily.

Teacher Eligibility Test

TET was introduced by the Government of India in the year 2011 to improve standards in teaching. The teachers already working were expected to pass the exam within 2 years.

The Government in India has implemented a teacher's eligibility test for teaching in schools (TET) under the National Curriculum Framework for Teacher Education. The primary objective was

Establish a national benchmark, standards for teacher quality and recruitment in schools and colleges.

Encourage further improvement in the performance standards of teacher education institutions and their students. To communicate the Government's particular focus on teacher quality.

These is the minimum eligibility criteria to become a government teacher in the state of middle schools. The tests are conducted mainly in two-level – Primary level (1-5Class) and Upper primary level for teaching (6-10Class) Now it has become mandatory to pass the TET exams to become eligible to teach in Government schools in India. The validity of the exams is 5 years for TET and 7 years for CTET.

The Eligibility in some of the state governments for eligibility as a teacher is 80% weight-age on DSE and 20% pass on TET. This gives scope in filtering and giving chance for underrated teachers in the state board school education System, which must be abolished immediately.

The standard of the schools is much lowered. This flaw has to be corrected, and eligibility must only be on TET /CTET examinations, and those who clear with at least 60% must be eligible to teach.

Some of the countries have a very high standard of tests, countries like Australia do not allow you to appear for the final semester in teaching graduation courses, and if the student does not clear the examination, he/she must change their teaching graduation stream in the University.

Teacher Professionalism and Remuneration.

The teacher-student ratio in many schools in the central & state government-run schools, the quality of education is much low compared to the countries in America and Europe. The right to education act (RTI) mandates an optimal student-teacher ratio of 30:1, where the performance of the students is affected badly in their assessments; the ration is much higher in India.

Another major concern in the state and government-run schools in the rural areas Is the absenteeism of teachers, which runs to about 25%, and the government is losing US$2.0 Bullion yearly on salaries payments as per the world bank estimates. Besides, the students' performance is getting affected.

Salary structure in the World.

The comparisons in terms of Rupee values with the developing countries are much lower, and the best talent is migrating to more lucrative countries.

There is also no system or motivation for the teaching staff in colleges and schools. Therefore the development

and learning skills are not upgraded due to lack of interest and motivation. Therefore we must have a system of yearly assessment based and skills and qualifications assessments linked to salaries and promotions. The organizational structure in the schools, which is currently a flat structure, must be replaced with a more robust hierarchal system of growth.

<u>Flat Hierarchy in School Management</u>.

<u>Current Teacher Hierarchy.</u>

City Council Head.

Principal of the School.

Teaching staff in schools.

<u>FLAT Hierarchy in school management-10</u>

The current structure in most of the Schools and colleges is flat evolved in the tenure and promotion review process, the no-growth prospects for the teachers.

Evaluation and Assessment of Teacher: To gain a true sense of our teaching- what's working and what isn't – takes a thoughtful and holistic approach. Such an approach is essential for not only ourselves but also everyone involved in the tenure and promotion review process, including the principal and the peers, to know how we're teaching effectively, taking feedback on the board, and focusing on continuous improvement.

We should value effective teaching and support instructions in exploring ways to improve their teaching skills, whether a new teaching assistant or a tenured teacher with distinguished teaching awards, we all have room for improvement, refinement, and experimentation with new ideas and learning technologies.

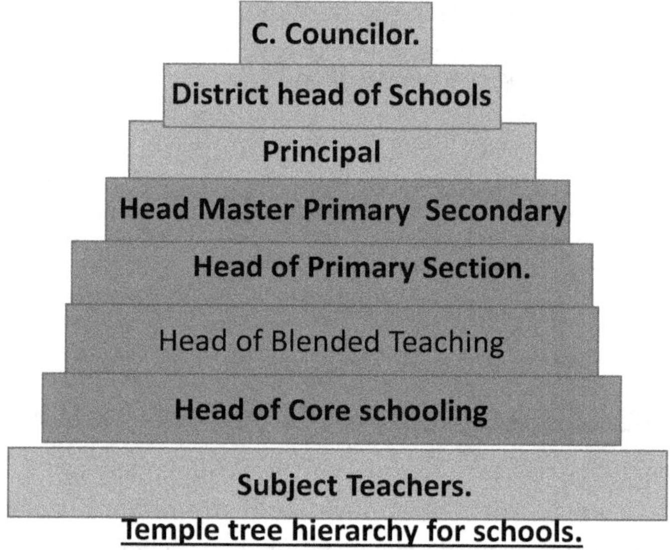

Multi-layer Hierarchy in Teaching -11

Self –reflection and constructive feedback from students, peers and the principal help instructors of all ranks discover if they are effective in the classroom and inform choices that improve the quality of teaching, sharing these insights with peers and Principal helps those colleagues know how best to support, mentor and promote instructors when it comes to teaching effectiveness.

Teacher's Eligibility Tests, Revised salaries structure, incentivize teachers for working in rural areas with additional perks. Yearly assessments linked to salaries revision have a growth path for teachers to reach higher levels in schools, will motivate the teachers to up their education and teaching skills, and will provide quality teachers in every region.

India is much lower in salaries to teachers, where we are not able to get the best-trained teachers, especially in rural areas and in state government-run schools.

Continues training for teachers to upgrade skills and impart the latest techniques and teaching methods is very important in the teacher's carrier.

Salaries, Rupee terms in the World-12 education.

Country	Average Annual Salary (In Rupees)
USA	41.44 lakh
Canada	53.97 lakh
Germany	33.18 lakh (starting)
Australia	31.15 lakh
England	26.23 lakh
India	2.01 lakh

Private stakeholders and Government funding:

The governments must increase the budget spending on the schools to improve their schools' standard of education, providing the best facilities and implement modern techniques of teaching in schools. Currently, many schools in poor nations spend about 2% to 4% of their GDP, which is very lower, which is not able to even sustain the basic infrastructure in schools. Many governments in Europe and America spent about 6% to 7% of their GDP. The government of India spends about 3.9% of the GDP, they have a proposal to increase the budget for education up to 6% of the GDP in the near future.

The new method of the reformation in schools, as suggested by Adaptive Modulation of Schooling, will substantially reduce the government's annual budget spend on education and also provides the best education to the students.

All state governments and corporation schools also have schemes that give free compulsory education up to 10th standard or 17 Years of age, in all government-run schools budget is shared by the central government and the state governments, with free mid-day meals also provided through Anganwadi centers.

Parents and Local leaders:

Social awareness and Elder trade skilling for self-reliance. In industry, Modern Farming, Dairy products, Live stocks, Hatchery, Fisheries, Horticulture, and Handicrafts to all those who have not gone through primary education, this gives an insight into the importance of education to the parents.

The influences in the homes and the local communities will become Influencers in a child's life once they are exposed to learning.

Parents who take on a supportive role in their children's learning make a difference in improving achievements and behavior. The amative involvement of parents can help promote a learning community in which children and young people can engage positively with practitioners and their peers.

PART VIII:

INDIA VISION FOR 21ST CENTURY IN EDUCATION:

The Educational sector In India:

To hasten, a host of reforms and improved financial outlays in recent years that could possibly transform the country into a knowledge haven. With human resource increasingly gaining significance in the overall development of the country, development of education infrastructure Is expected to remain the key focus in the current decade, in the scenario, infrastructure investment in the education sector is likely to see a considerable increase in the current decade.

The government of India has taken several steps, including the opening of IITs and IIM's in new locations, as well as allocating educational grants for researches scholars in most government institutions.

Furthermore, with the online mode of education being used by several educational organizations, the higher education sector in India is set for a major change and development in the years to come. – **Reference** – *press releases, press information bureau, RNCOS report.*

India Vision for the 21st Century of education: It is estimated that 2030 India's education will be

Combine training methods that involve online learning and games, and is expected to grow 38% in the next 2-4 years

Adapt transformative and innovative approaches in Higher Education.

Have an augmented Gross Enrolment Ratio (GER) to 50 % which is not 35% Reduce state-wise, gender-based and social disparity in GER to 5 %

Emerge as the single largest provider of global talent, with one in four graduates in the world being a product of the Indian higher education system among the top five countries in the world in terms of research output with an annual R&D spend of UD$140Billion. Have more than 20 universities among the global top 200 Universities.

Road Ahead for education initiatives in India:

The government promoted a new scheme, "Study in India' to bring foreign students to higher educational institutions.

To boost the Skill India Mission, two schemes, Skill Acquisition and Knowledge Awareness for Livelihood Promotion (SANKALP) and Skill Strengthening for Industrial Value Enhancement (STRIEV) have been approved by the Cabinet Committee on Economic Affairs (CCEA), Government of India, with an outlay of Rs. 6.655 crore(US$1.02Billion) will be supported by the world bank.

The Ek Bharat Shreshtha Bharat (EBSB) campaign is undertaken by the Ministry of Human Resource Development to increase engagement between states, union territories, central minister educational institutions, and the general public.

Major Initiatives are taken by the Government:

In May 2020, Government has launched PM eVIDYA, a programmer for multi-mode access to digital/online education. Other initiatives to be launched include Manodarpan, New National Curriculum and Pedagogical framework, National Foundational Literacy, and Numeracy Mission.

According to Union Budget 2020-21Government allocated Rs.59,845 Crores (US$ 8.56 Billion) for the Department of School Education and Literacy.

Revitalizing Infrastructure and Systems in Education (RISE)by 2022 was announced in Union Budget 2020-21 with a proposed outlay of Rs.3000 core (US$ 429.58 Million)

Union Budget 2020-21, Government proposed apprenticeship embedded degree/diploma courses by March 2021 in and about 150 higher educational institutions.

As of February 2020, 2,54,897 training centers were registered in India, and around 2 crore candidates completed training under the **Pradhan Mantri Gramin**

Digital Saksharta Abhiyan (PMGDISHA)---NDTV Education.

INDIAN Government's initiative of VidyaDaan by 2022.

Implement e-learning resource to Individuals, Teachers, Educationists, Entrepreneurs, Corporate, Government, and Non-Government Organizations, for any grade for K-12 on any subject.

The government encourages different types of e-learning resources as can be contributed.

PART IX:

NATIONAL EDUCATION POLICY -2020

*"New educational policy is based on the pillars of access, equity, quality, affordability, and accountability, transforms India into a vibrant knowledge hub." – **PM Modi.***

The new national education policy has been approved by the Union Cabinet and released by the government on 29th July 2020, this brings about major reformations in the education system after 34 years, there are many bold and drastic changes proposed in the policy, with some of the major shift from the existing policy in school and college education, if implemented in the right senses suggested in this book, it will propel India into a new Country with the generation of people having a better lifestyle, eradication of poverty and discriminations. some of the major changes proposed by the Government in the NEP-2020:

Early Childhood Care and Education-(ECCE) It is envisions universalization of early childhood education from 3-6 years of age by 2025. The new structure is to attain fundamental literacy and numeracy by class 3. A new coding and vocational studies from class 6 and a child's mother tongue being used as the medium of instruction till class 5 at primary education with trilingualism will have adhered to the choice of the students with at least two of the three languages are native to India. In contrast, foreign languages will be offered a the secondary level.

A new curricular framework is to be introduced, including the pre-school and Anganwadi years. A national mission on Foundational Literacy and Numeracy will ensure basic skills at the class 3 level by 2025. Students will begin classes on coding as well as vocational activities from class 6 onwards.

Teaching and Assessments: The new school structure is drawn out from K-12 with a range of 3 years to 18 years of student education. New stricture of 5+3+3+4, up to 5 years of age Pre-school, 6-8 Mid school, 9 to 12 High school, and 12 onwards Graduation. (New system 5 years of foundation education, 3 years of preparatory, 3 years of middle and 4 years of secondary schooling)

Bag-less days: School students to have 10 Bag-less days in a year during which they are exposed to a vocation of choice (Informal Internship)

Semester wise Examinations: All school exams will be semester wise twice a year. The board examinations will be made easier to test core competencies rather than memorized facts with all students allowed to take the exam twice.

Holistic Multidisciplinary Education: Bachelorette Degree will be of 4 years of study, with a multidisciplinary bachelor's program. The students can choose core study courses available to pursue till Graduations.

With flexible curricula, creative combinations of subject, integration of vocational education, and multiple entries and exit points with appropriate certifications. Or example certificate after 1 year, advance diploma after 2 years, Bachelor's degree after 3 years and Bachelor's with research after 4 years.

Other initiatives in the NEP-2020:

All higher education will be governed by only one Authority; UGC & AICTE will be merged to form a single board of higher education. The regulator – **Higher Education Commission of India – (HECI)** with verticals to form regulation standard-setting, grants, and accreditation. All Universities, private, Open, Deemed, Vocational, etc. will have the same grading and other rules. It will have multiple entry and exit from any course and award credits & certificates accordingly. For example, if the student completes 2 years course, he will be awarded a Diploma certificate, and if he completes 4 years course, he will be awarded a Degree certificate.

HECI will also function through faceless intervention through technology and will have powers to penalize higher education institutions for not conforming to standards.

The introduction of the four-year Undergraduate Program in Liberal Arts Science Education (LASE) is designed to develop broadly "useful capacities" (critical thinking, communication skills, scientific temper, social responsibilities, etc.) all universities and colleges must focus on becoming multidisciplinary by 2030.

In the course of time, Colleges will not need to seek affiliations but award degrees themselves. After the master's degree, there will be no MPhil before a Ph.D. A provision has also been made on allowing foreign universities to set up campuses in India.

Academic Bank of Credit (ABC):

The ABC will digitally store the academic credits earned from various recognized (HIE) Higher Education Institutes- so that a degree can be awarded, taking into account of the credits earned from any HEIs.

NEP-2020, Emphasizes, universal access to schools, and aim to bring two crore, out –of –school children, back into the educational mainstream. Aim is to double the gross enrolment ratio in higher education, from 26.8% to 50% by 2035. It proposes to raise the budget for education from 4.01% of GDP to 6 %. GDP

National Education Technology Forum (NETF)

NETF Will is created for the exchange of ideas on the use of technology to enhance learning, assessment, planning, and administration. The dedicated unit will be proposed for the creation of digital infrastructure, digital content, and capacity building, Integration of technology to improve classroom teaching. Support teacher's professional development, and enhance educational access for disadvantaged groups.

Financial support to meritorious students belonging to economically disadvantaged groups and those belonging to SC, ST, OBC's. Encourage stand-alone technical universities, health science universities, legal and agricultural universities to become multidisciplinary institutions. **Multidisciplinary Education and Research Universities (MERU)**

At par with IIT's and IIM's to be set up as models of best multidisciplinary education of global standards in the country.

Research Culture form Primary to higher education:

National Research Foundation (NRF):

NRF Will be created as an apex body for fostering a strong research culture and building research capacity across higher education.

On NEP-2020.-"There is an emphasis on aspects such as better infrastructure, innovative education centers to bring back dropouts into the mainstream, facilitating multiple pathways to learning among others". ***PM Mr. Narendra Modi***

PART X

INITIATIVES BY OTHER DEVELOPED COUNTRIES:

Some of the initiatives take by other countries like America, to boost the quality of education and freedom of choice to the parents, to educate their children in schools of their choice; the government is offering Educational Vouchers.

Education Vouchers for students in America: A school voucher is a credit given to parents who want to move their children from public school to a private school of their choosing, most voucher programs involve moving taxpayers money from public schools to private schools. There is nothing inherently wrong with sending your child to a catholic, Buddhist, or Islamic school, but public funds should not be used for that purpose. That fundamentally violates the separation of Church and state because states are being forced to fund religious education.

Voucher programs are actively harming the failing public schools' system; the solution detracts from our ability to have meaningful conversations about the need to spend more money on public education. As the much-needed funds for upgrading their infrastructure, when teacher shortages are rampant, class sizes are ballooning. The real need is to adequately fund public schools so that they can actually provide quality cost-free education for all. **Ref:Pulicschoolrevied.com**

The amount of funding the parents receive is based on what the schools typically get for each student each school year. The scheme was started in the year 1960 when the liberal academics began to argue that the racial inequalities in the current school system could not be adequately addressed through a residentially segregated public school system.

To encourage parents to take advantage of their children to study in the choice of their schools and affordability, to get their wards enrolled in private schools for quality education and results, the government offers Education Vouchers.

PART XI:

UNESCO-UIS SUSTAINABLE DEVELOPMENT GOAL 4.0 BY 2030.

4.1: By 2030, ensure that all **girls and boys complete free**, equitable, and quality primary and secondary education leading to relevant and effective learning outcomes.

4.2: By 2030, ensure that all girls and boys have access to **quality early childhood development, care, and pre-primary education** so that they are ready for primary education.

4.3: By 2030, ensure **equal access for all women and men to affordable** quality technical, vocational, and tertiary education, including university.

4.4: By 2030, substantially **increase the number of youth and adults** who have relevant skills, including technical and vocational skills, **for employment**, decent jobs, and entrepreneurship.

4.5: By 2030, **eliminate gender disparities** in education and ensure equal access to all levels of education and vocational training for the venerable, including persons with disabilities, indigenous people, and children in vulnerable situations.

4.6: By 2030, ensure that all youth and a substantial proportion of adults, both **men, and women, achieve literacy and numeracy.**

4.7: By 2030, ensure **all learners acquire knowledge and skills** needed to promote sustainable development and sustainable lifestyles, human rights, gender equality, promotion of a culture of peace and non-violence, global citizenship, and appreciation of cultural diversity and of culture's contribution to sustainable development.

4.7a. **Build and upgrade education facilities** that are child, disability and gender sensitive and provide safe, non-violent, inclusive and effective learning environments for all

4.7b: By 2020, substantially **expand globally the number of scholarships** available to developing countries, in particular, least developed countries, small island developing states and African countries, for enrolment in higher education, including vocational training, information and communications technology, technical, engineering and scientific programs, in developed countries and other developing countries.

4.7c: By 2030, substantially **increase the supply of qualified teachers,** including through international cooperation for teacher training in developing countries, especially the least developed countries and Small Island Developing States.

4.7c1: Proportion of teachers who have received at least the **minimum organized teacher training**

4.7c2: **Pupil –trained teacher ration** by education level

4.7c3: Percentage of **teachers qualified according to national standards** by education level and type of institution.

4.7c4: Pupil-qualified teacher ration by education level.

4.7c5: **Teacher attrition rate** by education level.

While governments hold the main responsibility for ensuring the right to quality education, the 2030 Agenda is a universal and collective commitment. It requires political will, Global and rational collaboration and the engagement of all governments, civil society, the private sector, youth, UN and other multilateral agencies to tackle educational challenges and build systems that are inclusive, equitable and relevant to all learners.

PART XII:

SUMMARY:

Blended Learning Schools:

Blended Learning in Schools: Combining IN-PERSON & ONLINE Learning, educational material and opportunities for interaction online with fabulous place-based, In-person classroom teaching for all classes from K-12 standard in schools and all undergraduates courses in collages, for theoretical and Metaphysics, Psychology learning & language learning subjects with up to 70% of their studies in blended teaching.

Core Learning Schools:

The method of Adaptive Modulating: 30% of learning in Core learning School at the specified periods from K-12, utilizing the facilities within a radius of 0-Km to 5-Km radius of Blended learning schools. (Student's Primary enrolled schools) *Bag-less learning schools – NEP-2020*.

Experimental & Experiential Learning:

Learn by reflecting on active involvement that provides facilities like, Laboratory, Outdoor Botanical gardens, Zoological classes in Zoo, Art and Theater, Museums, the core schools with these facilities of teaching, learning must be part of the curriculum of their course time. These are schools built to offer in their respective specialized fields of education, independently operating as profit centers. Example: A Botanical Garden with classrooms in the same complex to impart practical and live demonstration, similarly with other fields of study, it would be Sports Academy or Theater & Film institute.

Instructional Scaffolding Learning:

The support given to a student by an instructor taught the learning process and aid in mastering the tasks. The teacher does this systematically building on students' experience, knowledge, as they are learning new skills in Sports, Games, Swimming, Drill, YOGA, and Indoor, activate like Gymnasiums, Karate, and competitions can be held in schools especially made for utilizing these facilities. The schools can use their fixed time as per their curriculum of studies.

Transformative Learning Schools:

It is the process of Perspective transformation has three dimensions, Psychological (Change in the understanding of the self), Conviction (revision of belief systems) and Behavioral (lifestyle changes)

Meta-Similarity learning Schools:

Computer science and an area of supervised machine learning in artificial intelligence. It is closely related to regression and classification, but the goal is to learn from examples a similarity function that measures how similar or related two objects are

Autodidacticism Learning Schools:

Common Central library and Computer Centers with network can be set up for the reference of books and study material for all schools, making mandatory from Primary schooling onwards for children to become habitual, for self learning using facilities as common use, similar to other facilities, offered to the schools surrounding in a range of 0 KM to 5 KM radios.

The adaptive modulating system for the schools and colleges must be accordingly programmed depending on the stream of studies and the level of teaching the school or colleges are offering, they can vary the percentages of teaching as required for the courses.

Benefits of Adaptive Modulation Learning Schools and Colleges:

Adaptive modulation Schools are be built with infrastructure separately for core field of study, as mentioned with facilities like Sports Academy having Stadiums for Athletics, Gymnasiums, Sports, and Games with professional teachers and staff to impart the best teaching and coaching students, operating independently as a profit center.

Similarly, Schools and Colleges built with infrastructures for Labs, workshops for practical and hands-on training.

Blended Schooling with modern classroom infrastructures for teaching in-person classes and through online and media broadcasting, and on occasions where necessitates and facilities students for interaction with other students of the class and teachers, also for writing their board exams.

Equip children with laptops or Smart phones for online classes, classrooms with electronic boards, visual aids, etc.

Through this method of study, the student enrolled in Parent School, will be assessed and graded in consultancies with the CORE earning schools in their respective subjects obtained from different fields of study.

Elder's education system in India.

Education makes a significant difference for adults, particularly when it applies to day to day life, including nutrition, healthcare, and gender equality. When adults learn, they become role models to their children; even lactating mothers must be taught life-supporting skills (Knitting, Stitching, and Handicrafts & Pottery) in the Anganwadi Centers.

For those elders who wish to pursue higher education, there are various learning schools available.

Night Learning Schools. The existing Learning schools can be used by students who want to attend classes for various reasons in the night, similarly, as taught in a

Blended learning School for better imparting knowledge and learning.

Virtual learning: The limitations are the same as Home Schooling with no direct interaction with the teaching staff, socializing, games, or utility of Labs, whereas now with the CORE Learning Schools, the same facilities can be offered.

Distant education: The schools with the syllabus already provided, the student buys the books and learned by the students themselves. They can use guide books for assistance. Now using technology, they can learn through TV broadcasting, enroll in an ONLINE School. The dates for exams will be announced, and the student has to take tests at specified centers.

Brake – in - Year education: With the new policy NEP - 2020, a student can take brake in studies for various reasons. Also, it cannot continue, yet will be awarded yearly as per his completion of course, in the earlier studies, he would have lost the entire period of study for not completing the course.

Education at Lower Cost:

The Schools with poor funding or those mostly run by Government organizations and especially in remote locations, which lack infrastructure facilities, the students are deprived of excelling in their field of interest, as the school is not able to identify the talent In the students to nurture them to excel, therefore by sharing the infrastructure and facilities for the schools the opportunities available to students are enormous. The CORE schools specialized in their field of knowledge can concentrate and impart the best to the students.

Equal opportunities to all students, be it in Government or Private Schools, to excel in all subjects and activates and at reasonable costs, yet maintaining the students / School profile intact.

The purpose of the adaptive moderation of schooling is to give equal opportunity to the students in education and learning to their own maximum potential, which was lacking in the current system of education in many countries, and the great financial burden on the Governments and Educational boards.

The curriculum is set by depending on the board of education, followed in that particular school.

Teacher training and remunerations:

Some teachers do not have adequate qualifications and training to teach in many Government and Charitable institutions.

The absenteeism of teachers in schools is of grave concern. 25% of teachers are absent in schools, losing UD$2.Billion annually on salaries, as per World Bank. Students losing interest in studies and there learning classes, whereby their performance and grades are depleting year on year, depriving the students of their right to education and achieve success in life.

To achieve competency, teachers must pass with 60% in TET examinations, which are valid for 5 year period. The teacher assessments, upgrading of skills, and growth must be carried out as specified in earlier chapters.

A win-win situation for all stakeholders:

The Teachers, Students, Administrators, the Boards, Governments, Trustees, and Leaders in the education system are all benefited from the new module of the education system.

The core school infrastructure is shared by all schools in the nearby vicinity, for different fields of the learning depending on their enrolment in the subjects of interest, they can avail the best of the facilities qualified instructors.

The sharing of the infrastructure of the core schools, gives advantages in terms of specialization for the students and also the appointment of teaching & support staff, as of now there are many schools which are strong in specific studies or games, for example, schools with no sports grounds or physical education teachers, generally do not participate in such activates, nor excel.

All CORE teaching schools (In the Grid) must be independent and operate separately, schools with all the modern facilities, tools, and aids suitable for teaching the school's curriculum, with a professional approach using support staff and administrative management for operating as profit centers.

Honest implementations of these structure specified will bring great results in schools, the students will be empowered with the knowledge required to reach the panicle of their lives, eradicate discrimination and live better life in socially.